A Variety of Exciting Fashion Designs for Teens & Adults

Coloring Pages for the Fashion-Mad

COPYRIGHT

This Book Belongs to

_____

_____

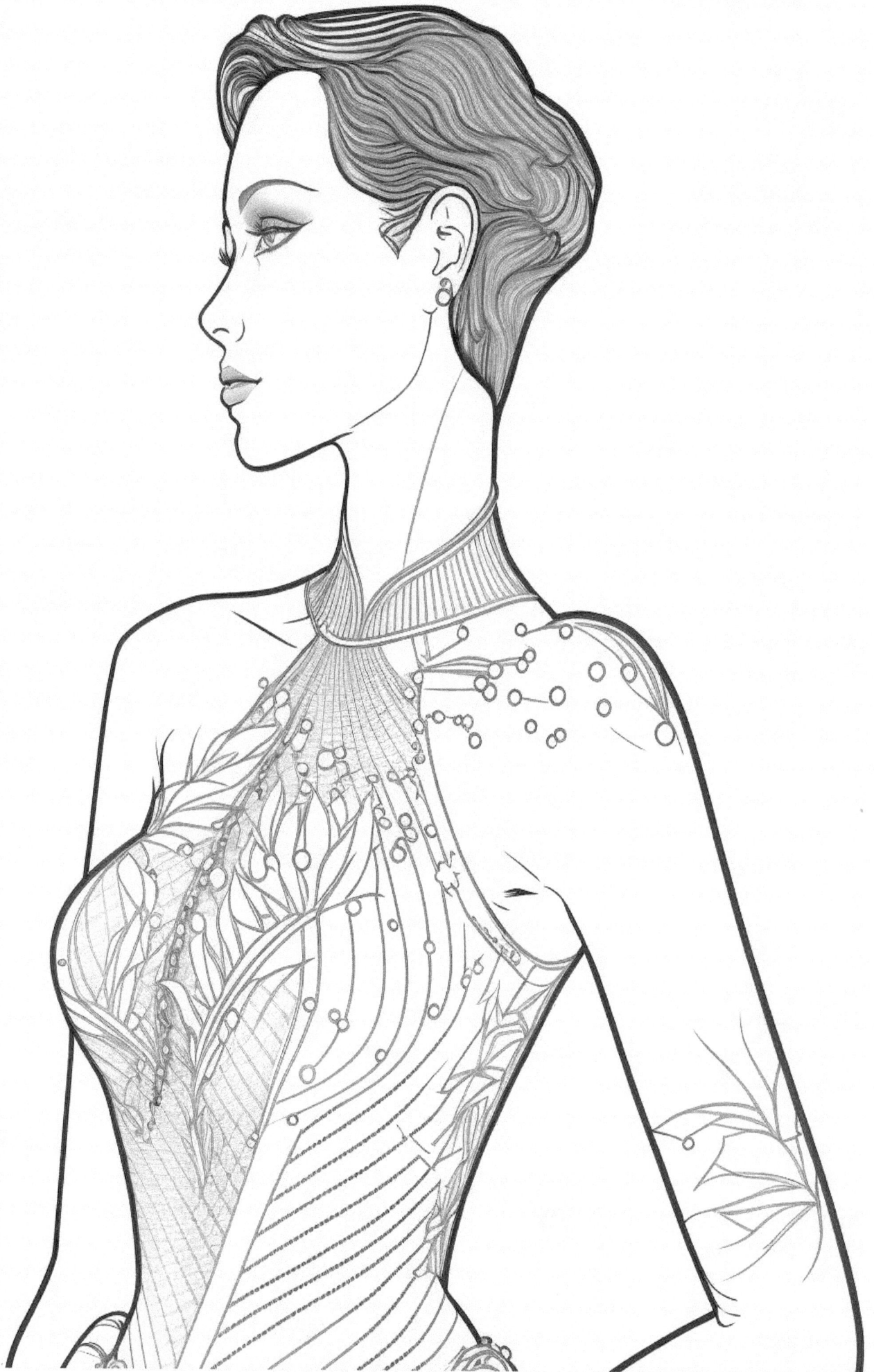

Thank you for buying this book!

If you liked it, please leave an honest review.
It would be much appreciated.

Other Books Published by JMSD Publishing Limited

CHILDREN'S BOOKS

Horse Mad 4-8 Year Old Kids' Coloring Book – Book One
Horse Mad 4-8 Year Old Kids' Coloring Book – Book Two
Horse Mad 8-12 Year Old Kids' Coloring Book - BookThree

New Skills for 3-6 Year Olds - Cursive Handwriting
Practice Workbook

Brain Teaser Puzzles – Word Search, Sudoku & Mazes

Create the Greatest Action, Adventure
Comic Book of Your Own - Blank Comic Book

Japanese Hiragana and Katakana Practice Exercise Book A4

Squared Notebook A4 Softcover: Leather Effect Cover

BOOKS FOR ADULTS

Adult Coloring Book - 50 Beautiful & Original Patterns – Mandalas,
Animals, Birds & Insects

Everyday Cook's Recipe Book for Family Favourites - Blank Recipe
Book

My Fishing Log Book

The Keen Gardener's Log Book & Journal: For Planning, Designing,
Establishing & Maintaining a Beautiful Garden –
52 Week Gardening Log Book

Aged Notebook A4: Old Style Notebook Interior - Lined
Vintage Notebook - 100 Pages, Wide Lined Exercise Book
Leather Effect Cover